Extreme Snowboarding Moves

By Jeri Freimuth

Consultants:
Greg Johnson
World Wide Development
International Judges Commission
Olympic Half-pipe Head Judge
Nagano, Japan

Scott W. Flanders
Media Coordinator
U.S. Ski and Snowboard Association

CAPSTONE
HIGH-INTEREST
BOOKS

an imprint of Capstone Press
Mankato, Minnesota

Capstone High-Interest Books are published by Capstone Press
151 Good Counsel Drive, P.O. Box 669, Mankato, Minnesota 56002
http://www.capstone-press.com

Library of Congress Cataloging-in-Publication Data
Freimuth, Jeri.
 Extreme snowboarding moves/by Jeri Freimuth.
 p.cm.—(Behind the moves)
 Includes bibliographical references and index.
 ISBN 0-7368-0784-5
 1. Snowboarding—Juvenile literature. [1. Snowboarding. 2. Extreme
sports.] I. Title. II. Series.
GV857.S57 F74 2001
796.9—dc21   00-009843

Summary: Discusses the sport of extreme snowboarding, including the moves
involved in the sport.

Editorial Credits
Angela Kaelberer, editor; Karen Risch, product planning editor; Kia Bielke,
     cover designer and illustrator; Katy Kudela, photo researcher

Photo Credits
AB/Photographers/Aspen, 4 (inset)
Allsport USA/Brian Bahr, 7; Al Bello, 21 (top), 24; Elsa, 27
Bobridges.com, cover, 18, 21 (bottom)
Brian Bailey/Photographers/Aspen, 4, 8, 10, 10 (inset)
Burnham W. Arndt/Photographers/Aspen, 24 (inset)
CK Photography, 14, 15 (bottom), 20
Mark Gallup/Pictor, 19
Mark Turner, 16, 22
Patrick Batchelder, 15 (top)
Sean Sullivan/FPG International LLC, 13 (bottom)
Visuals Unlimited/Mark Gibson, 13 (top)
W. Lynn Seldon, Jr., 16 (inset), 28

1 2 3 4 5 6 06 05 04 03 02 01

Table of Contents

Learn about:

- **Types of snowboarding**
- **Snowboard parks**
- **Equipment**

Chapter One

Freestyle Snowboarding

People first used snowboards in the early 1980s. At first, snowboarders simply rode their boards down ski slopes.

Many skateboarders became interested in snowboarding by the mid-1980s. These skateboarders began performing skateboarding tricks on snowboards. This type of snowboarding became known as freestyle snowboarding.

Freestyle riders perform tricks in snowboard parks. These parts of ski areas are set aside for snowboarders. Snowboard parks contain jumps made of snow and obstacles such as railings.

Jumps and Pipes

Snowboard park jumps are called straight jumps or kickers. These mounds of snow are 1 to 10 feet (.3 to 3 meters) high.

In competitions, freestyle riders perform tricks on straight jumps. They also perform in half-pipes or quarter-pipes made of snow. Half-pipes have two curved walls. The curved area of each wall is called the transition. Half-pipe walls are separated by a flat area. Most half-pipes are 7 to 17 feet (2.1 to 5.2 meters) high and 328 feet (100 meters) long.

Quarter-pipes have only one wall. They are about 20 feet (6.1 meters) wide. Most are the same height as half-pipes.

Both half-pipes and quarter-pipes have a top edge. This edge is called a lip. Riders often perform tricks above the lip.

Types of Snowboarding

Freestyle is one type of snowboarding. The other main types are alpine and freeride. Alpine snowboarders race down mountains. Freeride snowboarders ride on open slopes at ski areas or in remote mountain areas.

Some freeride snowboarders compete in Boardercross events. Six riders race on downhill courses that include straight jumps, banked jumps, and turns. Banked jumps are built-up areas of snow. Riders sometimes bump and crash into each other as they race to the finish.

Half-pipes have two curved walls.

Snowboarding Equipment

Snowboards are made of strong, lightweight materials. Some are made of carbon fiber or fiberglass. Others are made of layers of wood that are glued together. Most freestyle boards are made of a combination of wood and

Snowboards are made of strong materials.

fiberglass. Fiberglass boards bend easily during tricks. Wood gives the boards strength.

All snowboards have some common features. Snowboards have metal edges that help them cut through snow. Bindings hold the rider's feet on the board. The snowboard's front is called the nose. The back is the tail.

Snowboards are measured in centimeters. They can be 100 to 200 centimeters (39 to 79 inches) long and 15 to 30 centimeters (5.9 to 12 inches) wide. Most freestyle boards are about 150 centimeters (59 inches) long and 24 to 25 centimeters (9.4 to 9.8 inches) wide. The board's short length allows riders to spin quickly through the air during tricks. The board's wide width helps riders balance. It also provides a more secure landing than a narrow board does.

Snowboarders wear hard or soft boots depending on what type of riding they do. Racers wear hard boots that give them more support as they carve through snow. Freestyle riders wear soft boots. These boots allow riders to move easily as they perform tricks.

Some snowboarders ride goofy foot.

Learn about:

- **Riding position**
- **Ollies and nollies**
- **Slides, straight airs, and grabs**

Chapter Two

Basic Tricks

Many freestyle riders also ride skateboards. Many basic freestyle snowboard tricks are based on skateboard tricks.

Riding Position

Snowboarders ride the half-pipe either frontside or backside. They face the wall when riding frontside. Their backs are to the wall when riding backside.

Riders can ride their boards regular or goofy foot. Riders who ride regular have their left foot in front. Goofy-foot riders place their right foot in front. A rider's foot position determines which side of a ramp wall is frontside and which is backside. For regular riders, the right-hand side of the wall is frontside and the left is backside. The opposite is true for goofy-foot riders.

Riders perform some tricks and jumps fakie or switch. When riding fakie, riders' feet are in the opposite position of how they usually ride. Riders who ride switch have both feet centered directly across from each other on the board. They can take off on either foot as they do tricks.

Ollies and Nollies

Riders perform ollies and nollies to jump over obstacles and to jump on railings. To begin an ollie, riders bend their knees and shift their weight to their back foot. They spring off the snowboard's tail. They then stand up and bring their front knee to their chest. To do a nollie, the rider springs off the snowboard's nose.

Slides

Many snowboard parks have rails that look like handrails on stairs. Riders perform an ollie or nollie to get on the rail. They then slide down. They call this trick a rail slide or board slide.

The most popular slide tricks are the 50/50 slide and the Smith grind. Riders perform a 50/50 slide by sliding the board lengthwise along the rail. During a Smith grind, the rider slides sideways along the rail. The board's nose is angled below and the tail is angled above the rail.

Riders also perform nose or tail slides. They balance the board's nose or tail on the obstacle as they slide.

Ollie

Riders perform slides on rails.

13

Straight Airs

Snowboarders perform some basic aerial tricks in half-pipes. A jump without any flips or spins is called a straight air.

Frontside and backside airs are the most common straight airs. These airs are performed on either the ramp's backside or frontside wall.

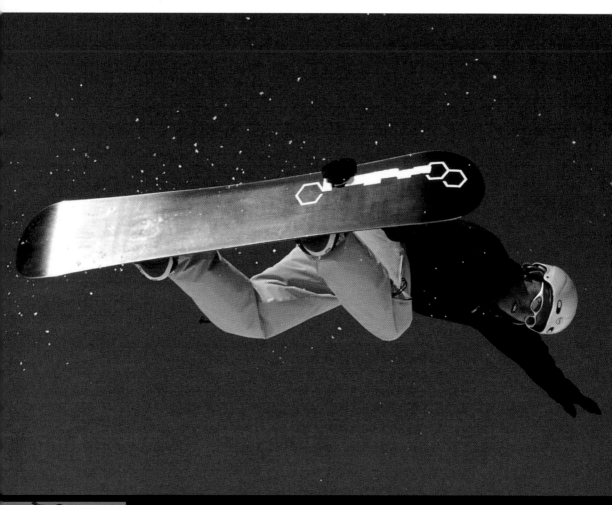

The method air is a popular grab.

The side of the wall depends on whether they are riding regular or goofy foot. Riders keep their legs bent as they soar through the air. They straighten their legs as they land.

Grabs

Riders often grab their snowboards as they perform straight airs. This adds difficulty and style to the trick.

The method air was one of the first snowboarding grabs. It still is popular today.

Riders begin a method air by riding up the half-pipe's backside wall. They pull the board behind their back as they jump above the ramp's lip. Riders arch their body and grab the board's heel edge with their front hand.

Riders perform hundreds of types of grabs. Riders sometimes do nose or tail grabs. They grab the board's toe edge as they jump. They may do mute grabs. These riders grab the board's toe edge with their front hand. Riders also perform stalefish grabs. They use their back hand to grab the snowboard's backside edge between the bindings.

Frontside air

Stalefish grab

15

Flips are vertical rotations.

Learn about:

- **Flips and spins**
- **Handplants**
- **Combination tricks**

Chapter Three

Advanced Tricks

Expert freestyle snowboarders move on to advanced tricks such as aerials. Riders spin through the air or turn themselves upside down as they perform these rotations.

Flips

Flips are vertical rotations. Riders rotate straight through the air as they do flips.

Riders do front and back flips off straight jumps. These tricks are called inverts. A single flip is an inverted 360. A double flip is an inverted 720. Riders also perform inverts in half-pipes. They flip their bodies over when they reach the lip. Some riders learn flips on trampolines. They then try the tricks in half-pipes.

Spins are horizontal rotations.

Spins

Spins are horizontal rotations. Riders rotate sideways through the air as they do spins.

Riders perform spins off straight jumps. One full turn is a 360. A 540 is a full turn plus a half turn. A 720 is two full turns. Some expert riders even do 900s and 1080s. These riders make two-and-a-half or three turns in the air.

Handplants

Riders sometimes put one or both hands on the lip as they do inverts. Riders call these tricks handplants. Riders can perform handplants on the half-pipe's frontside or backside wall.

Some handplants include rotations. An Andrecht handplant is a backside

handplant with a 360. But few riders
do handplants in competition. They would
rather do more difficult tricks such as
inverted aerials with rotations.

Riders perform handplants on half-pipe walls.

Combination Tricks

Expert snowboarders combine flips, spins, and grabs into tricks. A rodeo flip is an inverted 540 backflip spin on the backside wall. A McTwist is an inverted 540. It combines a forward flip on the backside wall with a mute grab.

The rodeo flip is an inverted 540.

The McTwist combines a flip and a grab.

Some tricks are named after the people who invented them. Norwegian rider Terje Haakonsen invented the Haakonflip. This trick is an inverted 720 aerial that combines a 360 flip with a 360 spin. Riders begin the trick riding fakie. They rotate backside as they become inverted.

Haakonflip

Extreme Snowboarding Slang

air—a trick performed in the air

bail—to fall

bone—to straighten one or both legs during
a trick.

fall line—the straightest path down a hill or slope

flat—the area between a half-pipe's transitions

goofy foot—to ride with the right foot in front;
normal position is left foot in front.

grommet—a young snowboarder

session—time spent snowboarding

switch—to ride with both feet centered on
the board

Learn about:

■ **Safety equipment**

■ **Clothing**

■ **Safety rules**

Chapter Four

Safety

Snowboarders were not welcome in many ski areas during snowboarding's early days. Skiers thought snowboards were dangerous. Early snowboards were hard to control. This caused problems at some ski areas.

Today, most ski areas allow snowboarders to ride throughout the ski area. Most also have snowboard parks. Riders can practice their tricks in these areas. But riders still need to follow safety rules.

Safety Equipment and Clothing

Safety equipment can help protect riders. Many riders wear helmets to protect themselves from being hurt during falls. In many competitions, riders must wear helmets. Riders also wear goggles to protect their eyes. Goggles reduce the glare caused by the sun's rays reflecting off snow.

Snowboarders also need proper clothing. In cold weather, riders should wear several lightweight layers of clothing.

Layers of clothing help prevent riders from losing body heat. Loss of body heat can cause hypothermia. This condition occurs in most people when their body temperature drops below 95 degrees Fahrenheit (35 degrees Celsuis). People who have hypothermia may become confused and sleepy. They may even die.

Layered clothing also allows riders to control their body temperature. Riders can remove or add layers as they become too warm or cold. Riders also should wear gloves to keep their hands warm.

The top layer of riders' clothing should be waterproof. This protects riders against frostbite. Frostbite occurs when cold temperatures freeze skin. The skin tingles, loses feeling, and turns white. People may lose the use of frostbitten fingers, toes, arms, and legs.

Goggles protect riders' eyes.

Helmets help keep riders safe.

Staying Safe

Snowboarding has changed since the early 1980s. Riders do more dangerous tricks and ride in more dangerous places.

Beginning riders should take lessons to learn how to snowboard safely. Most ski areas and snowboard parks offer snowboarding lessons.

Beginning riders also can stay safe by knowing their limits. Riders should stay inside snowboard parks until they are able to ride well. They should learn basic moves before trying tricks.

All riders should learn basic tricks before trying advanced ones. They should wear safety equipment and follow safety rules. By doing these things, snowboarders can practice safe snowboarding and still have fun.

Words to Know

aerial (AIR-ee-uhl)—a trick performed in the air

binding (BINE-ding)—a fastener that holds a rider's feet on the snowboard

fakie (FAY-kee)—to ride or perform a trick opposite of the usual position

hypothermia (hye-puh-THUR-mee-uh)—a condition that occurs when a person's body temperature falls several degrees below normal

obstacle (OB-stuh-kuhl)—an object that stands in a rider's way; riders sometimes perform tricks on obstacles.

rotation (roh-TAY-shuhn)—a trick in which snowboarders spin at least 360 degrees in the air

transition (tran-ZISH-uhn)—the curve of a ramp between the flat area and the walls

To Learn More

Kidd, P. J. *Snowboarding: Big Air and Boarder X.* The Extreme Games. Edina, Minn.: Abdo, 1999.

McKenna, Anne T. *Big-Air Snowboarding.* Extreme Sports. Mankato, Minn.: Capstone High-Interest Books, 1999.

Ryan, Pat. *Extreme Snowboarding.* Extreme Sports. Mankato, Minn.: Capstone High-Interest Books, 1998.

Useful Addresses

Association of Ontario Snowboarders
1580 Trinity Drive, Unit 14
Mississauga, ON L6T 5L6
Canada

United States of America Snowboard Association
P.O. Box 3927
Truckee, CA 96160

United States Ski and Snowboard Association
P.O. Box 100
1500 Kearns Boulevard, Building F
Park City, UT 84060

Internet Sites

International Judges Commission

http://www.I-J-C.de

Nova Scotia Snowboard Association

http://www.nssa.ca

Snowboarding-Online.com

http://www.snowboarding-online.com

United States Ski and Snowboard Association

http://www.ussnowboard.com

Index